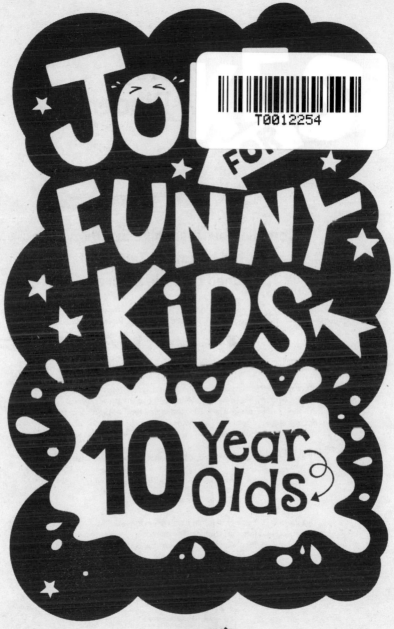

JOKES FOR FUNNY KIDS

10 Year Olds

BUSTER BOOKS

Illustrated by
Andrew Pinder

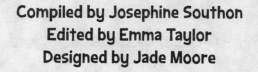

Compiled by Josephine Southon
Edited by Emma Taylor
Designed by Jade Moore

First published in Great Britain in 2023 by Buster Books, an imprint of
Michael O'Mara Books Limited, 9 Lion Yard, Tremadoc Road, London SW4 7NQ

W www.mombooks.com/buster   f Buster Books   🐦 @BusterBooks   📷 @buster_books

A CIP catalogue record for this book is available from the British Library.

ISBN: 978-1-78055-965-0

1 3 5 7 9 10 8 6 4 2

This product is made of material from well-managed, FSC®-certified
forests and other controlled sources. The manufacturing processes conform
to the environmental regulations of the country of origin.

This book was printed in August 2023 by
CPI Group (UK) Ltd, Croydon, CR0 4YY.

FSC
www.fsc.org

MIX
Paper | Supporting
responsible forestry
FSC® C171272

CONTENTS

Introduction
What did the pirate say on his 80th birthday?

"Aye matey!"

Welcome to this te he he-larious collection
of the best jokes for 10-year-olds.

In this book you will find over 300 side-splitters,
which will have you howling with laughter,
from animal roarers and travel teasers to gross
gags and knee-slapping knock-knocks!

If these jokes don't tickle your funny bone
then nothing will. Don't forget to share them
with your friends and family and rehearse
your comic timing, too!

GROSS GAGS

Did you hear about the skunks who fell in love?

It was love at first fart.

Why did the zombie take a sick day?

It was feeling rotten.

Why did the fart miss graduation?

It got expelled.

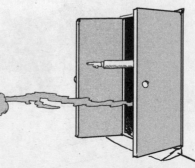

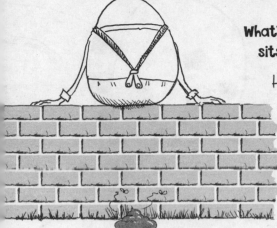

What's big, brown, and sits behind a wall?

Humpty's Dump.

What's the most musical part of your body?

Your nose, you can blow it like a trumpet and pick it like a guitar.

What's the smelliest card game?

Top Trumps.

What do snowman bogies taste like?

Carrots, of course!

Two Australian birds burped in my face ...

... I wasn't emu-sed.

What do you call a smelly fairy?

Stinkerbell.

What did the bogey say to the finger?

"Pick on someone your own size!"

Why was the hoodie so smelly?

Because it was a heavy sweater.

What do you call a bogey in space?

An astro-snot.

What did one fart say to the other during the quiz?

"Your gas is as good as mine."

395   423

Why did the skeleton burp?

It didn't have the guts to fart.

What did one bogey say to the other?

"You think you're funny, but you're snot."

Where are poo criminals taken?

To the dung-geons.

What's invisible and smells like carrots?

Bunny burps.

What did one flea say to the other?

"Shall we walk or take the dog?"

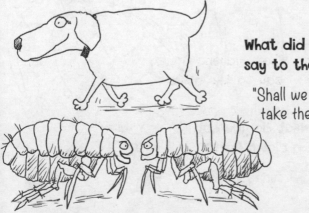

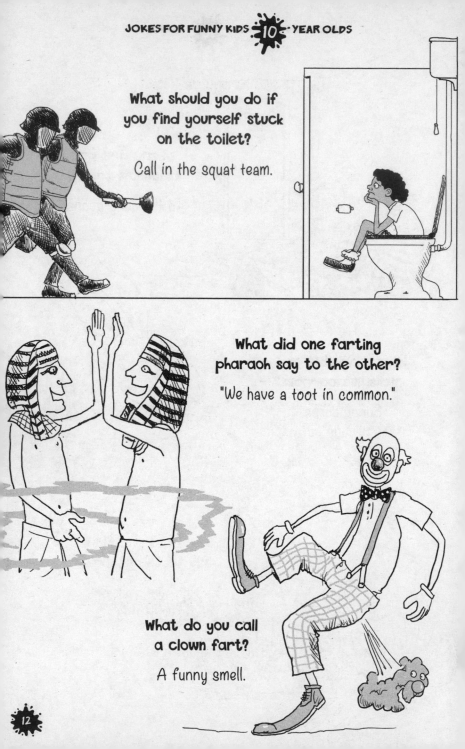

What should you do if you find yourself stuck on the toilet?

Call in the squat team.

What did one farting pharaoh say to the other?

"We have a toot in common."

What do you call a clown fart?

A funny smell.

What's brown and sticky?

A stick ... What were
you thinking of?!

**Why is it difficult to
have a conversation
with a butt?**

It's always butting in.

**What did the nose say when
the person sneezed?**

"I'm coming down with something."

What do you call a pile of frog poop?

Toad-stools.

Who does the world's most dangerous farts?

Ninjas. Their farts are silent, but deadly.

Why does Piglet smell?

Because he's always playing with Pooh!

How do you fit more pigs on your farm?

Build a sty-scraper.

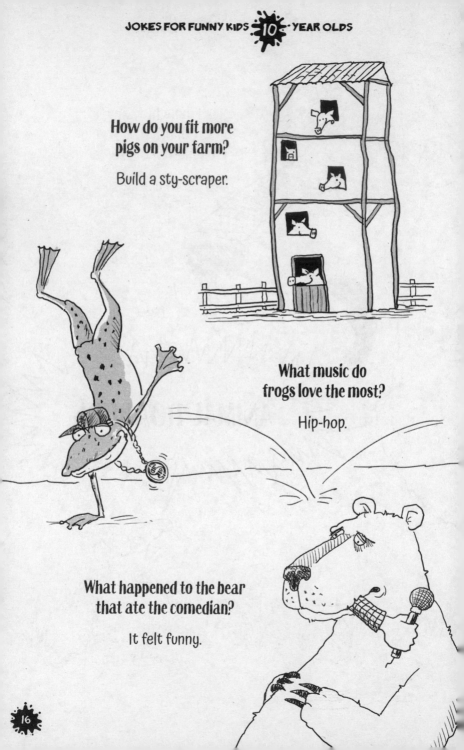

What music do frogs love the most?

Hip-hop.

What happened to the bear that ate the comedian?

It felt funny.

I thought taking off
a snail's shell would
make it move faster ...

... But it made it sluggish.

Why do elks love jokes?

They like being amoosed.

What do you get when
you cross a hammock
with a dog?

A rocker spaniel.

17

What sound do porcupines make when they kiss?

Ouch!

What kind of bird works at a construction site?

A crane.

What does a turtle do on its birthday?

It shell-ebrates!

How does a cat know
when it's going to snow?

It checks the weather fur-cast.

What do you call an ape
who wins all the awards?

A reigning chimpion.

Why did the pig have
ink on its face?

It came out of its pen.

Which bird is always sad?

A blue jay.

Why do seagulls live by the sea?

Because if they lived by
the bay, they'd be bagels.

**Why did the cat go
to medical school?**

To become a first-aid kit.

Which fish only swim when it's dark?

Starfish.

Have you ever seen a catfish?

No I haven't, how did it hold the fishing rod?

Which dog breed loves baths?

A sham-poodle.

Why do dogs run in circles?

Because it's hard to run in squares!

Why was the dog bad at dancing?

It had two left feet.

How does a mouse feel after a shower?

Squeaky clean.

What do you call a monkey wearing headphones?

Anything you like, it can't hear you!

Which American state has a lot of cats and dogs?

Pet-sylvania.

What do ducks buy for fireworks night?

Firequackers.

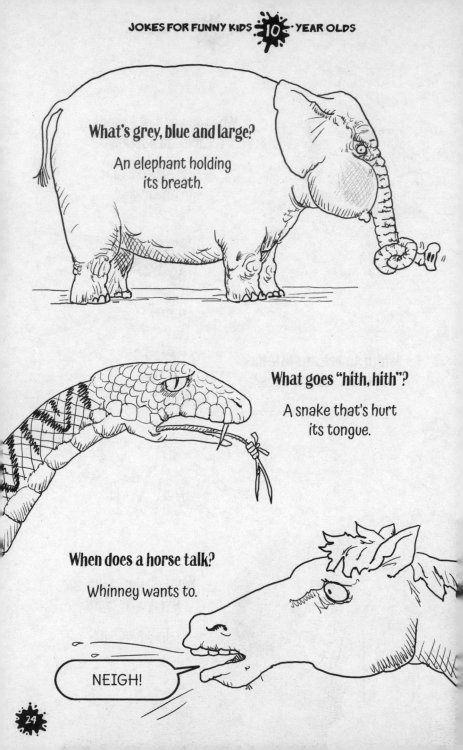

What's grey, blue and large?

An elephant holding its breath.

What goes "hith, hith"?

A snake that's hurt its tongue.

When does a horse talk?

Whinney wants to.

NEIGH!

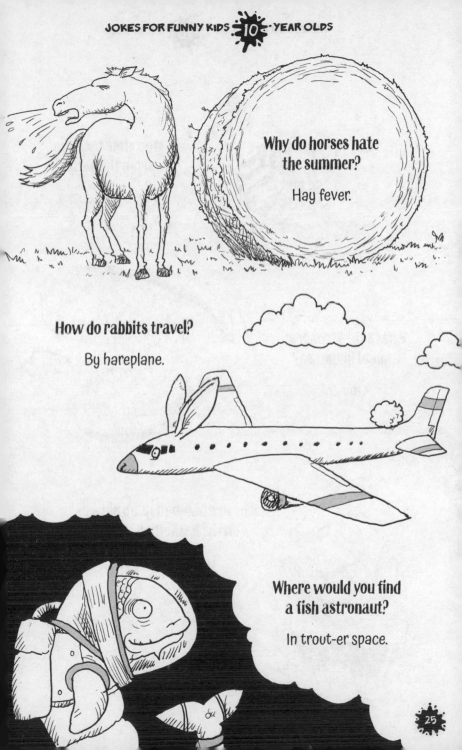

Why do horses hate the summer?

Hay fever.

How do rabbits travel?

By hareplane.

Where would you find a fish astronaut?

In trout-er space.

Who stole the soap from the bath?

The robber ducky.

What's the strongest animal in the sea?

A mussel.

Why are pigs bad team players on the basketball court?

They hog the ball.

Which dog breed is guaranteed to laugh at your jokes?

A chi-ha-ha.

What wears glass slippers and weighs over 4,000 pounds?

Cinderellephant.

How do owls communicate?

They wing each other.

27

What's black, white and red all over?

A sunburnt zebra.

Which animal does Dracula love most?

A bloodhound.

Why are monkeys terrible storytellers?

They only have one tail.

How do you stop a bull from charging?

You unplug it.

What dessert do cats love the most?

Chocolate mouse.

How do bees get to school?

By school-buzz.

"My dog has no nose."

"How does it smell?"

"Awful!"

What does a kitten say
when it gets hurt?

"Me-oww!"

What do you get if you cross
a pig with a T. rex?

Jurassic Pork.

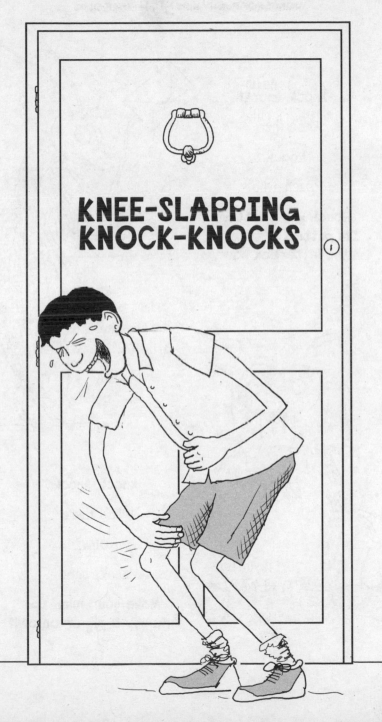

KNEE-SLAPPING
KNOCK-KNOCKS

Knock, knock!

Who's there?

Roach.

Roach, who?

Roach you a letter,
I'm putting it through
the letterbox now.

Knock, knock!

Who's there?

Oink.

Oink, who?

Make your mind up.
Are you a pig or an owl?

Knock, knock!

Who's there?

Hal.

Hal, who?

Hal will you ever find out if you don't open the door?

Knock, knock!

Who's there?

Hawaii.

Hawaii, who?

I'm good thanks, how are you?

Knock, knock!

Who's there?

Olive.

Olive, who?

Aw, olive you, too!

Knock, knock!

Who's there?

Theodore.

Theodore, who?

Theodore wasn't open
so I knocked!

Knock, knock!

Who's there?

Somebody who's too short to ring the doorbell.

Knock, knock!

Who's there?

Iva.

Iva, who?

Iva sore hand from knocking, let me in!

knock, knock!

Who's there?

Iran.

Iran, who?

**Iran here, now
I'm tired.**

knock, knock!

Who's there?

Cash.

Cash, who?

**No thanks, but I'd
love some peanuts.**

Knock, knock!

Who's there?

Nana.

Nana, who?

Nana your business!

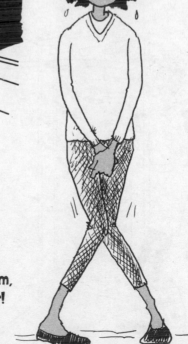

Knock, knock!

Who's there?

Anita.

Anita, who?

Anita use the bathroom, please open the door!

Knock, knock!

Who's there?

Ivor.

Ivor, who?

Ivor you let me
in or I'm climbing
through the window.

Knock, knock!

Who's there?

Sue.

Sue, who?

Sue-prize party,
happy birthday!

Knock, knock!

Who's there?

Nobel.

Nobel, who?

Nobel ... that's why I knocked!

Knock, knock!

Who's there?

Pecan.

Pecan, who?

Pecan someone your own size.

Knock, knock!

Who's there?

Dragon.

Dragon, who?

How many dragons do you know exactly?

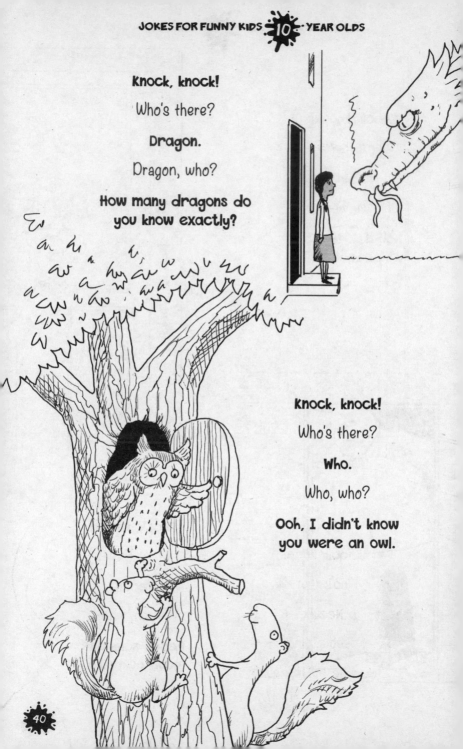

Knock, knock!

Who's there?

Who.

Who, who?

Ooh, I didn't know you were an owl.

Knock, knock!

Who's there?

Alec.

Alec, who?

Alec-tricity - BUZZ!

Knock, knock!

Who's there?

Needle.

Needle, who?

Needle little help
out here!

What sport do insects love the most?

Cricket.

Why did the golfer wear two pairs of shorts?

In case he got a hole in one.

Why did the baseball team hire a baker?

They needed a new batter.

What animal is best at hitting a cricket ball?

A bat.

What are the rules for zebra baseball?

Three stripes and you're out.

What sport does Mickey Mouse love the most?

Minnie golf.

I kept wondering why the baseball was getting bigger ...

... And then it hit me.

How do top players keep cool?

They stand near the fans.

When does a British tennis tournament end?

When it's Wimble-done.

What do soccer players like to drink?

Penal-tea.

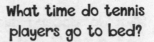

What time do tennis players go to bed?

Tennish.

How do soccer players deal with their problems?

They tackle them.

Why is Cinderella never picked for the team?

Because she's always running away from the ball.

What do soccer players
on the naughty list get
for Christmas?

COOOAAALLL!

Where do tennis
players go to dance?

The tennis ball.

What sport do wasps
love the most?

Sting Pong.

What's the hardest part of skydiving?

The ground.

What do cheerleaders eat for breakfast?

Cheerios!

What do you call a boomerang that doesn't come back?

A stick.

What sport are waiters really good at?

Tennis, because they serve so well.

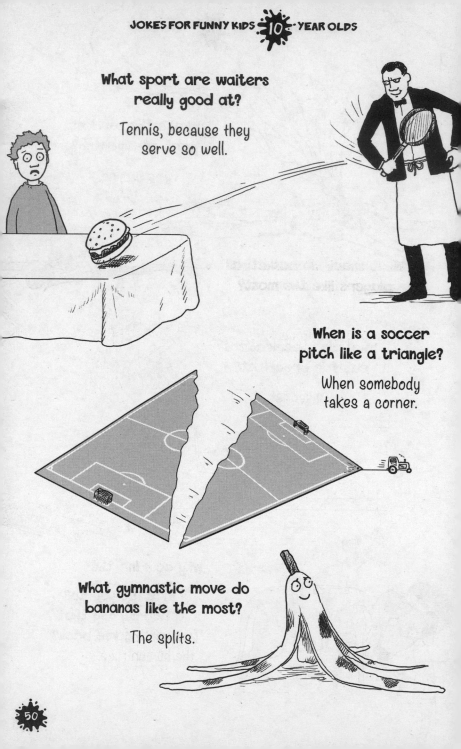

When is a soccer pitch like a triangle?

When somebody takes a corner.

What gymnastic move do bananas like the most?

The splits.

What's something you serve, but can't eat?

A tennis ball.

What snack do basketball players like the most?

Milk and cookies, they love to dunk.

Why couldn't the dog take part in the marathon?

It wasn't part of the human race.

I had to sell my rowing boat ...

... It was oar-full.

50%

What lights up a soccer stadium?

A soccer match.

What sport do elves like the most?

Boxing.

Why can't you play dodgeball in the jungle?

There are too many cheetahs.

Why is tennis such a loud sport?

Because the players make a racquet.

SILLY SCIENCE

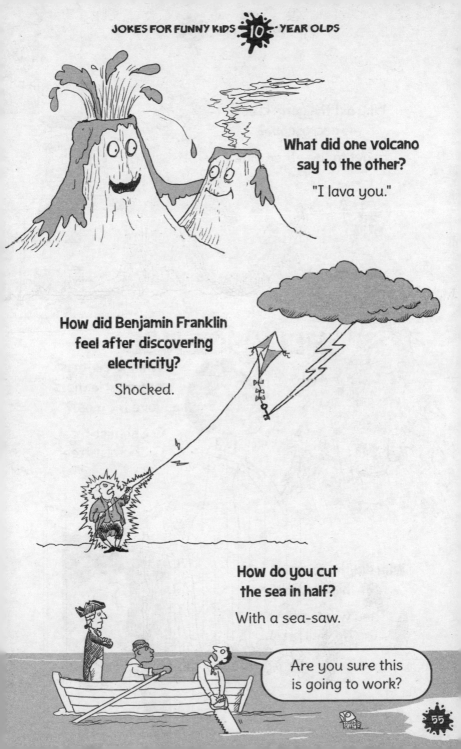

What did one volcano say to the other?

"I lava you."

How did Benjamin Franklin feel after discovering electricity?

Shocked.

How do you cut the sea in half?

With a sea-saw.

Are you sure this is going to work?

Why did the germ cross the microscope?

To get to the other slide.

What Christmas song do scientists love the most?

O Chemist-tree!
O Chemist-tree!

Why did the scientist take out their doorbell?

They wanted to win the No-bell prize.

Why did the computer keep coughing?

It had a virus.

What kind of photos do cells take?

Cell-fies.

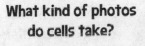

I told a chemistry joke the other day ...

... There was no reaction.

What do astronauts serve dinner on?

Flying saucers.

How do you stop an astronaut's baby from crying?

You rock-it.

Why is electricity the perfect student?

It conducts itself well.

How much room do fungi need to grow?

As mushroom as possible.

What kind of dogs do chemists have?

Laboratory Retrievers.

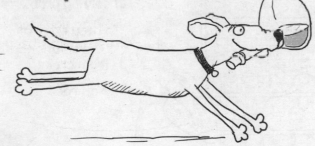

What element do pirates love the most?

Arrr-gon.

What do you call an acid with an attitude?

An a-mean-oh-acid.

Why are chemists great at solving problems?

They have all the solutions.

What food do physicists love the most?

Fission chips.

Renewable energy is great ...

... I'm a big fan.

What did the biologist wear during fashion week?

Designer genes.

What do skeletons say before dinner?

"Bone appétit!"

Where do wizard scientists work?

In a labracadabratory.

What did the flower say to its parent?

"Don't leaf me!"

Where do Earth scientists like to relax?

In rocking chairs.

TRAVEL TEASERS

What's the best thing about Switzerland?

I don't know, but the flag is a big plus.

Which city never stops moving?

Rome.

Where's the best place in the world to see sharks?

Fin-land.

Which Californian city is known for its dancing?

San Fran-disco.

What's the coldest place on Earth?

Chile.

What do grumpy mountains have?

Bad altitudes.

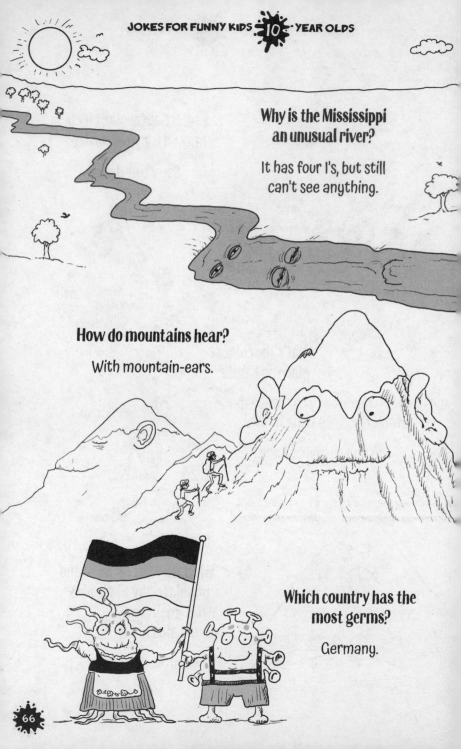

Why is the Mississippi an unusual river?

It has four I's, but still can't see anything.

How do mountains hear?

With mountain-ears.

Which country has the most germs?

Germany.

What stands
in New York all
day sneezing?

The St-achoo!
of Liberty.

What happened to the man who
took the 5 pm train home?

He had to give it back.

What do you call an island
populated by apple pies?

Dessert-ed.

Where can you find the biggest rope in the world?

Europe.

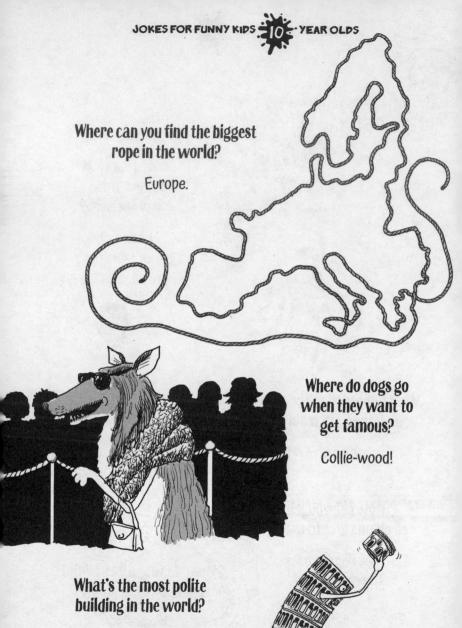

Where do dogs go when they want to get famous?

Collie-wood!

What's the most polite building in the world?

The Leaning Tower of Please-a.

If you drop a white t-shirt in the Red Sea, what will it become?

Wet.

Where do you find an ocean without water?

On a map.

How can you tell elephants love to travel?

They always pack their own trunk.

Which American state sneezes the most?

Mass-achoo!-setts.

Which part of a river is the richest?

The river-bank.

What did the teacher say when he finally found his map of the world?

"Atlas-t."

Where does the American president send their dirty laundry?

Wash-ington.

What's the tallest building in the world?

The library, it has the most stories.

Who is Mississippi married to?

Mister Sippi.

What do you call Finland's borders?

Finnish lines.

Child: Dad, where are the Andes Mountains?

Dad: At the end of your armies.

What dessert can you find roaming the Arctic?

Moose.

Why did the Moon orbit the Earth?

To get to the other side.

Teacher: What can you tell me about the Dead Sea?

Student: Dead? I didn't know it was sick!

Which Chinese city always cheats in exams?

Peking.

Why did the witch stay at the hotel?

She'd heard they had lovely b-rooms.

What's Australia's best-selling drink?

Coca-Koala.

What country do pirates like most?

Arrrgentina!

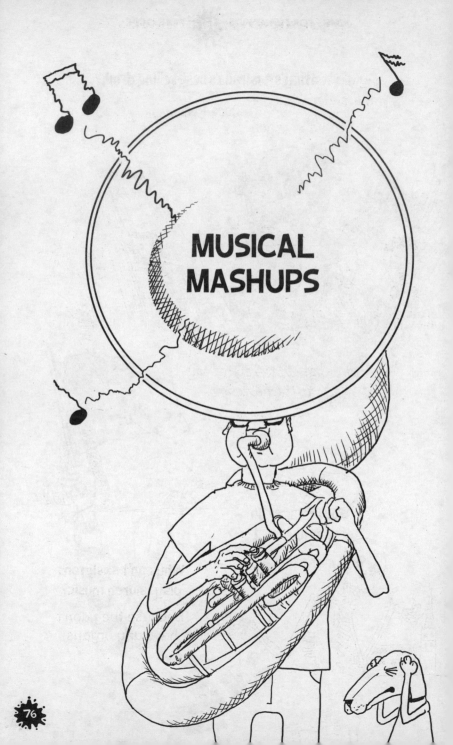

MUSICAL
MASHUPS

Why did the boy sit on the ladder to sing?

He wanted to reach the high notes.

What did the guitar say to the musician?

"Stop stringing me along!"

Why can't skeletons play church music?

Because they don't have any organs.

Why did the tortilla chip start dancing?

Someone put on some salsa.

How do you fix a broken brass instrument?

With a tuba glue.

What is Beethoven doing now?

De-composing.

What makes music in your hair?

A hairband.

Which parts of a turkey are musical?

The drumsticks.

How do you make a bandstand?

Take away their chairs.

79

What music should you listen to when you're fishing?

Something catchy.

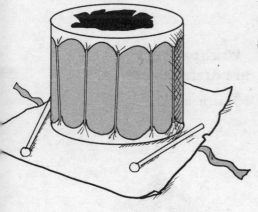

What's the best gift to buy a musician?

A broken drum, you just can't beat it.

What music can you play at lunch?

Wrap.

What do you call a musical insect?

A humbug.

Why do fish make great pianists?

They really know their scales.

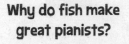

What's big, grey and has horns?

An elephant marching band.

What did the piano-playing magician say?

"Pick a chord, any chord."

What do you call a musical Christmas elf?

A wrapper.

What music do balloons like the least?

Pop!

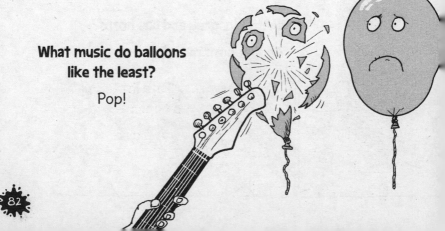

What musical instrument do skeletons like the most?

The trom-bone.

What did the conductor say to the triangle player?

"Thank you for every ting."

What has a lot of keys, but can't open any doors?

A piano.

**How does the Sun
listen to music?**

On the ray-dio.

**What music do avocados
like the most?**

Guac 'n' roll.

What music do robots love the most?

Heavy metal.

What does a witch play music on?

A broom-box.

Why do fishermen enjoy singing?

They love a good tuna.

I'm thinking about taking up woodwind lessons ...

... The bassooner the better.

What do cats like to dance to?

Meow-sic.

Why did the burglar rob the music shop?

For the lute.

What kind of band doesn't make music?

A rubber band.

What key do cows sing in?

Beef flat.

What do you call a jedi in an orchestra?

Oboe-wan Kenobi.

What do you call a music competition that's out of control?

Band-emonium.

What was the shortest lesson in the Stone Age?

History, there wasn't much of it.

Is that it?

Where did cave people eat breakfast?

Breakfast club.

Who did cave people go to when they needed help with counting?

A woolly mam-math.

1, 2, 3!

Caveman 1: Why do we always eat snails?

Caveman 2: Too much fast food is bad for you.

What did the caveman say to his son?

"Give me a big ugg!"

Why did the mammoth have a woolly coat?

It would have looked silly in a sweater.

How did Vikings send secret messages?

Norse code.

When a knight was killed in battle, what sign did they put on his grave?

Rust in peace!

What dog do Vikings like the most?

A Great Dane.

92

How many Anglo Saxons did it take to change a lightbulb?

None, there was no electricity back then.

Where was Henry VIII crowned?

On his head!

What happened to the soldier that lost his ear in battle?

He was never heard of again.

Why did the Viking buy an old boat?

He couldn't a-fjord a new one.

Which queen was always thirsty?

Elizabeth the Thirst.

Why were Vikings good singers?

They could reach the high Cs.

What did Vikings read to their children at bedtime?

Norse-ry rhymes.

What do you call a Viking on a plant-based diet?

A Nor-vegan.

Which fish do gladiators like to eat?

Sword-fish.

Who built King Arthur's round table?

Sir Cumference!

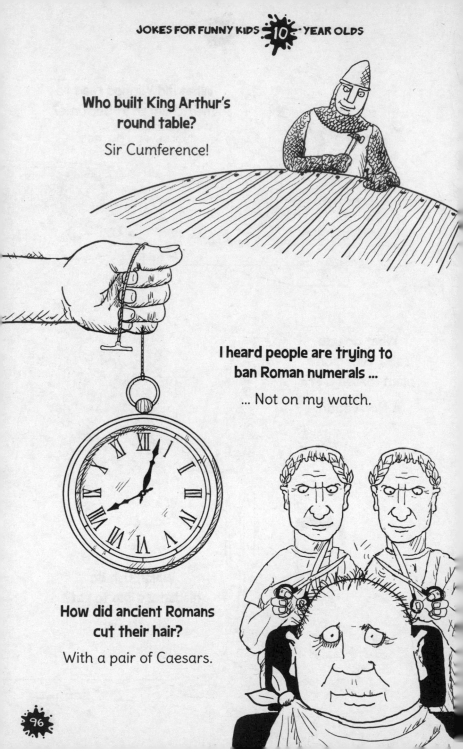

I heard people are trying to ban Roman numerals ...

... Not on my watch.

How did ancient Romans cut their hair?

With a pair of Caesars.

Where would you find Hadrian's wall?

At the bottom of his garden.

Where did the Russian Tsar Ivan the Terrible get his coffee from?

Tsarbucks!

What did one Roman emperor say to another?

"Toga-ther we can rule the world!"

Which pharaoh played the trumpet?

Tooting-khamun.

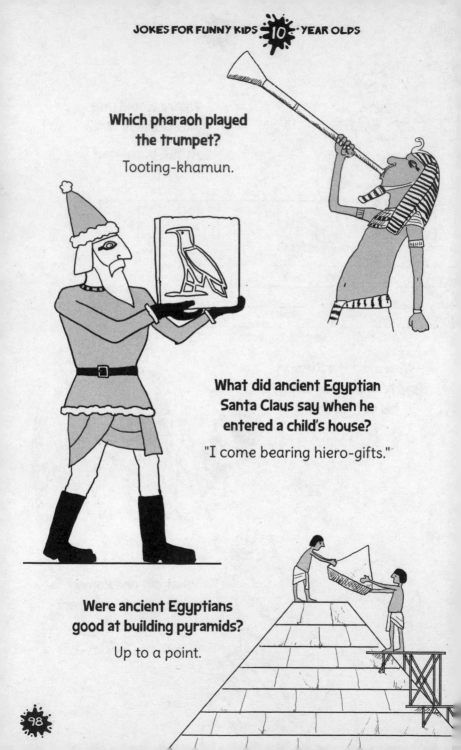

What did ancient Egyptian Santa Claus say when he entered a child's house?

"I come bearing hiero-gifts."

Were ancient Egyptians good at building pyramids?

Up to a point.

What were homes in ancient Crete made from?

Con-Crete.

Why didn't the philosopher like old French fries?

They were made in ancient grease.

What was the most popular movie in the ancient Greek city of Troy?

Troy Story.

Knock, knock!

Who's there?

Queen.

Queen, who?

Queen this kitchen, it's filthy!

What do you call a Roman emperor with the flu?

Julius Sneezer.

Who was hired to sweep chimneys in the Victorian era?

Anyone who was soot-able.

**Why was Queen Victoria
soaking wet?**

She reigned for
almost 64 years.

**How did Queen Victoria
respond to jokes?**

"I am not amused."

**What was the first thing
Queen Victoria did when
she came to the throne?**

She sat down.

RANDOM RIB-TICKLERS

How do bees brush their hair?

With a honeycomb.

My dog ate all of my Scrabble tiles ...

... He keeps leaving me messages around the house.

What did the pirate wear on Halloween?

A pumpkin patch.

Every morning I plan to make pancakes ...

... But I keep waffling.

What did the digital clock say to the grandfather clock?

"Look, no hands!"

Why did the baker put the cake in the freezer?

It needed icing.

Why did the student wear glasses in mathematics class?

It improved their di-vision.

What did the pirate say on his 80th birthday?

"Aye matey!"

How many apples grow on a tree?

All of them.

Why did the man fall down the well?

Because he couldn't see that well.

Where do boats go when they're sick?

To the dock.

Why did the teddy bear skip dessert?

It was stuffed!

What do you call a nervous sword fighter?

Shake-speare.

Where can you find a cow with no legs?

Right where you left it.

What did the teacher say when the book fell on their head?

"I only have my shelf to blame."

Why did the toilet paper roll down the hill?

To get to the bottom.

Why did the sandwich go to the dentist?

It had lost its filling.

What happened when two artists took part in a competition?

It ended in a draw.

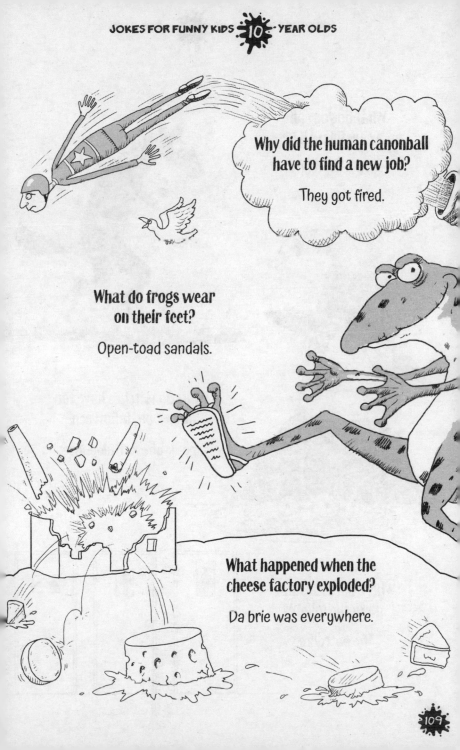

Why did the human canonball have to find a new job?

They got fired.

What do frogs wear on their feet?

Open-toad sandals.

What happened when the cheese factory exploded?

Da brie was everywhere.

What do you call a careful wolf?

An aware-wolf.

What do witches have for dinner on Halloween?

Spook-ghetti Bolognese.

Where does Batman go to the toilet?

The batroom.

What did one tomato say to the other?

"Catch up!"

How do hens stay fit?

They eggs-ercise.

What do you call a magician who's lost his magic?

Ian.

What do you call a dinosaur that can't see?

A Do-you-think-he-saw-us.

Why did the worker get fired from the calendar factory?

He took two days off.

Why are male ants good at swimming?

Because they're buoy-ants.

What did the family say when they lost some of their roof?

"Oof."

Why do people tell actors to "break a leg"?

Because every play has a cast.

Which day of the week are eggs scared of?

Fry-day.

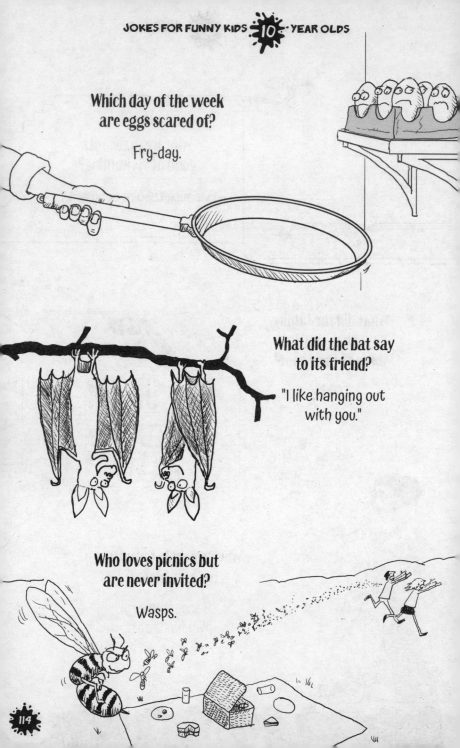

What did the bat say to its friend?

"I like hanging out with you."

Who loves picnics but are never invited?

Wasps.

Waiter, Waiter! Will my pizza be long?

No, it will be round.

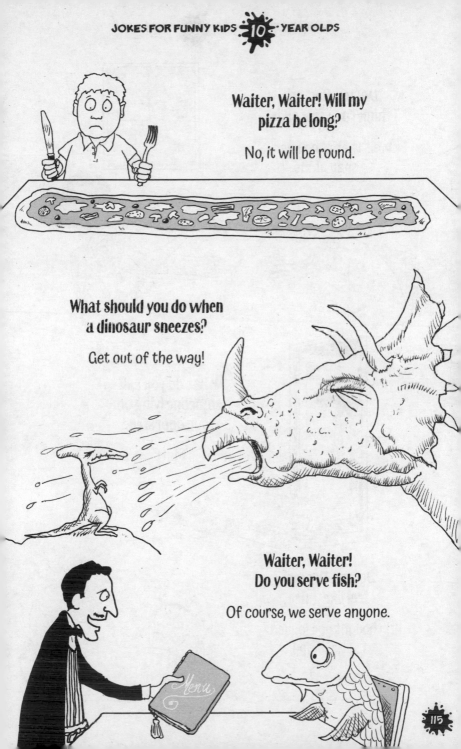

What should you do when a dinosaur sneezes?

Get out of the way!

Waiter, Waiter! Do you serve fish?

Of course, we serve anyone.

**Doctor, Doctor!
I think I'm a crocodile!**

Well, there's no need
to snap at me.

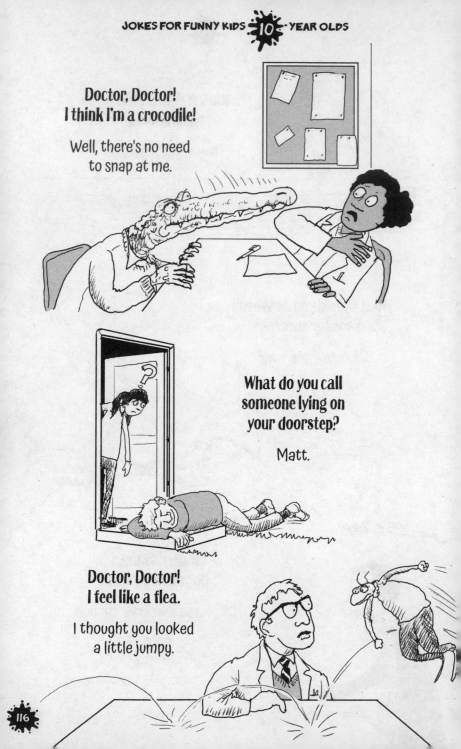

**What do you call
someone lying on
your doorstep?**

Matt.

**Doctor, Doctor!
I feel like a flea.**

I thought you looked
a little jumpy.

What do you call a fish wearing a top hat and a bow tie?

So-fish-ticated.

What do you call a dinosaur who knows lots of words?

A Thesaurus.

Did you hear about the man who almost drowned in a bowl of muesli?

A strong currant pulled him under.

What did the chef
give his partner on
Valentine's day?

A hug and a quiche.

Why don't mountains
get cold in winter?

Because they
have snow caps.

I can only remember
25 letters of the alphabet ...

... I just don't know y.

What do you call a helicopter with a cold?

A heli-coughter.

How do crows stick together?

With velcrow.

What is it like to ride in a hot-air balloon?

It has its ups and downs.

Why did the star go to school?

To get brighter.

How do you know when the Moon has had enough to eat?

When it's a full Moon.

What do planets like to do in their spare time?

Read comet books.

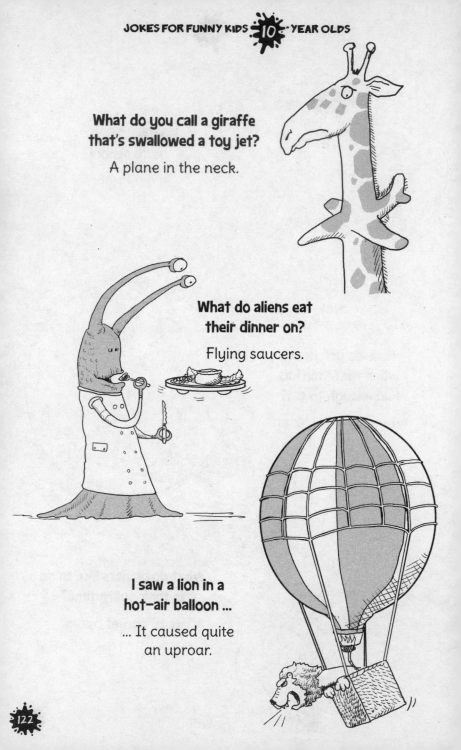

What do you call a giraffe that's swallowed a toy jet?

A plane in the neck.

What do aliens eat their dinner on?

Flying saucers.

I saw a lion in a hot-air balloon ...

... It caused quite an uproar.

How does Cupid travel long distances?

By arrow-plane.

Why did the alien go to the doctor?

It was looking a little green.

How did the bird fly without being spotted?

It was in di-skies.

How do birds learn to fly?

They don't, they just wing it.

What do you call an alien starship that's upset?

A crying saucer.

What happens if you wear a watch on a plane?

Time really flies!

Which planet likes accessories?

Saturn, it has seven rings.

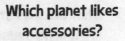

What drink do alien's like the most?

Gravi-tea.

What is it called when it's raining ducks and geese?

Fowl weather.

What did the astronaut find in his saucepan?

An Unidentified Frying Object.

What does a cloud do when it has an itch?

It finds the nearest skyscraper.

What do we want?

Plane noises.

When do we want them?

NNNEEEOOOWWW!

What do you get when you cross an astrophysicist with a tennis player?

A racket scientist.

What kind of spacecraft does Santa Claus ride?

A U-F-Ho ho ho.

How does a bird land safely with a broken wing?

With its sparrow chute.

ALSO AVAILABLE:

ISBN: 978-1-78055-963-6   ISBN: 978-1-78055-626-0   ISBN: 978-1-78055-624-6

ISBN: 978-1-78055-625-3   ISBN: 978-1-78055-964-3   ISBN: 978-1-78055-943-8   ISBN: 978-1-78055-908-7

ISBN: 978-1-78055-907-0   ISBN: 978-1-78055-785-4   ISBN: 978-1-78055-784-7   ISBN: 978-1-78055-708-3